What is self love?

Self-love is not about going through life thinking you are the best at everything. Narcissism and self-love are two completely different things and should never even be mentioned in the same sentence (except in sentences like this). Self-love is not about human perfection, nor is it about being flawless or above others. Self-love is not about instant gratifications, quick wins nor about a momentarily reaching an emotional or physical high.

Self-love is about respecting yourself knowing full well you deserve wellbeing and happiness. In the same loving way you feel about your partner, your sibling, or your friend, self-love is about directing that same feeling towards yourself, taking care of yourself, and being there for yourself. Self-love is about giving your body, brain, and mind the necessary fuel it needs to conquer the marathon of life. Having a balanced life where you and your well being are front and centre.. When you accept and love yourself you will start appreciating that every person's so-called weaknesses are what makes us who we are, and even they should be loved and accepted. When looking to your own needs instead of sacrificing your well being for others, you are practicing self-love. Self-love should be a lifelong practice, an inner muscle we constantly need to work out, and the best gift you can give yourself.

When in doubt, always treat yourself kindly.

Self-love

[/ˌself ˈləv/]   •   noun

● ●

Regard for one's own well-being and happiness.

How to use this book

This book will provide you with daily activities for you to move closer and closer to self-love. To love yourself, to treat yourself, and learn how to have a great time by yourself. We recommend doing one activity per day, but there is no right or wrong way to do it. Find your favorites to keep for later, skip some activities if you feel like it, or do them all in one fantastic week - it is up to you because this is your journey.

Some of the activities in this book might feel foreign or unnatural for you to do, especially if you have neglected yourself for a while, but hang in there! It will feel more natural as time passes, and sooner than you think your mind will start working with you instead of against you. You will start seeing the world from a different perspective.

Hopefully, this book is only the beginning for you, I hope that this book will set you on an adventure to truly change the way you look and feel about yourself.

You are the most important person in your life.

Take care of yourself.

Why This book?

As children, we are taught what to do, what not to do, how to socialize and make others comfortable, how to fit in with our peers, and gain their affection, but we were never taught to love, appreciate, and respect ourselves.

The human psyche is riddled with self-doubt, feelings of guilt, shame, and self-hate. I say enough of that! I say we deserve better from ourselves, and towards ourselves.

If you have had enough too really jump into this book, and fall in love with the person that matters most. You!

"You're always
with yourself, so
you might as well
enjoy the
company."

- Diane von Furstenberg

CALMING AND SMOOTH FACE MASK

SKIN TYPE:
NORMAL/DRY
TOTAL TIME:
15 MIN

INGREDIENTS

1 tablespoon Greek yogurt
1 teaspoon oatmeal
1 teaspoon honey

DIRECTIONS

Mix together all ingredients and apply on clean skin, and leave it for 10 to 15 minutes. Then rinse it off with warm water.

Remember to always do a patch test 24 hours before applying the face mask to your face.

Let's get serious

If you loved yourself fully, how would that make you feel and what could be different?

Dream and dream big - imagine a life in which you completely love yourself. Think of what ways your life could be different if you just accept yourself.

What is stopping you from having that life?

The dream life you just imagined is not at all impossible. The first step towards that life, is to figure out what the barriers are that are hindering you from that ideal. Do not rush this exercise. Think of all the barriers in your way, be it self confidence issues, being a people pleaser, or whatever else it might be, and try to write them all down so you easily get an overview of what work there is to be done.

What fulfills your life?

Knowing what it is that fulfills you in life is incredibly important. Most of our lives we have been taught to fit inside of a certain box, ideals of a dream life, and a dream job have been drilled into us. Most of us have never had the time to think to ourselves what is it that we enjoy in life. What do we find fulfilling?

If we are a banker with an artist's heart we can never be happy unless we have an outlet for our creative side.

Stop neglecting your inner self. Find out what it is that matters most to you - what you enjoy most in life, and use it to pick yourself up when life feels hard so you'll always have something that you enjoy and can fall back on.

Letting go of anger or sadness

We all have hurt in life and a lot of times our hurt can stay with us for a rather long time. When we hold on to emotions of anger, pain, and hurt it can easily wear us down. This exercise is tailor-made for releasing these pent up toxic emotions.

Write it and let it go

Write a letter to someone that has made you feel or is currently making you feel negative emotions. Write to get the negativity up, stand up for yourself, feel for yourself, and have your voice be heard! It is up to you if you want to show the letter to the person, save it for yourself, or simply get rid of it. We are only doing it to release our pent up emotions so write whatever it is you want to write. Do not think about the person on the other side, and do not censor yourself.

This exercise can be done as many times as you want. Good luck!

Letter to:

_____

_____

_____

_____

_____

_____

_____

_____

_____

_____

_____

_____

_____

_____

_____

"No one can make you feel inferior without your consent."

- Eleanor Roosevelt

PICK ME UP MANGO SMOOTHIE

**TOTAL TIME:
10 MIN**

INGREDIENTS

1 cup Peaches
1 cup Mangoes
1 Banana1 cup
Orange Juice
1/4 teaspoon Turmeric
1/4 teaspoon Ginger

DIRECTIONS

Add the ingredients into a blender and blend until smooth and creamy. Add ice depending on temperature preference.

Frozen bananas work best in smoothies so I recommend peeling, slicing, and placing your bananas in a large Ziploc bag in the freezer overnight before adding them to your smoothie.

Be Fair
No Apologies
Stick to Values
Be Truthful

Daily action

Every day you are making a ton of different choices, choices that can either build yourself up or tear yourself down slowly. Choose consciously and willingly to engage in behavior that builds yourself up, and abandon all the little choices made because you do not think you are good enough.

If you want to start making healthy choices that build you up you need to be more aware of the motivation behind your actions, which is easier said than done. Abiding by the FAST formula is the best way to go about this. This tried and tested guide when followed results in happier people with a healthier sense of self-respect.

F - be fair to yourself and treat yourself as you would treat others.

A- don't apologize for yourself when it is not necessary. Just because you have a different outlook on something doesn't mean that is wrong. Hold your head high.

S- don't compromise to please others especially if it means you have to betray yourself to do it.

T- be honest and don't exaggerate. We often make excuses and tell white lies so we do not feel like we are less in front of others. This can do lasting damage to your self-confidence and sense of self. In other words, do not be afraid to tell people the honest truth about yourself.

WHO AM I?

In this exercise, you are going to remind yourself of what a unique and fantastic being you are. Write down all the things, traits, strengths, quirky things you like about yourself. Be creative and don't leave anything out.

This might feel very unnatural for some of you, but it is mostly because we have never learned how to care about and respect ourselves like we do others. This exercise is here to force you to do just that.

Feel free to go back to this exercise and add words, whenever you are reminded of new amazing things about yourself.

declutter
=
happier you

Why declutter?

You might ask yourself why on earth this book is telling you to clean. Wasn't this book about self-love? You are correct, it is, but we are going to tackle self-love from a number of different angles. A lot of research has shown that you feel happier, more relaxed, less stressed, more focused, more productive, and confident by keeping your living space tidy and organized. Our external life often reflects our internal life and vice versa. Other research shows that the act of decluttering itself fires parts of your brain that reduce anxiety and leaves you in an overall more positive mood.

1 2 3 action

This book does not intend for you to become a full-blooded minimalist, the point is simply to get your brain to think a bit differently, and for you to create new and better habits. A good first start to a more decluttered life is to get rid of things you don't need and give it to a charity. Decide on a number of things you want to donate first. Decide right now before starting this exercise. Does 10 sound good? Or are you ballsy enough to go for 15? It is completely up to you. Once you have decided, go through your home and closet and don't stop until you have found as many items as the magic number you picked. If the items require washing or cleaning, do so, and then go drop them off at the nearest charity or second-hand shop.

You have now cleaned up your place a bit, felt a little satisfied, and gave something at the very low cost of nothing! Repeat this exercise as many times as you want! I personally love doing this once a month.

" *Love yourself first and everything else falls into line. You really have to love yourself to get anything done in this world.*"

— Lucille Ball

GLOWING AND FRESH BODY SCRUB

SKIN TYPE:
NORMAL/DRY
TOTAL TIME:
5 MIN

INGREDIENTS

1/2 cup sea salt
1/2 cup oil of your
choice
essential oils (optional)

DIRECTIONS

Mix all the ingredients together and apply on skin. Gently massage your skin with the scrub for 2 minutes and rinse off with warm water.

Let's talk

What do you need to feel more at peace with yourself?

List the most obvious answers, but think about it deeply and give it some time, no need to rush. Some answers might surprise you! Only when you understand what you need is inner peace within reach.

Exercises like are important so we become aware of our problem, and the destination we want to get to.

How can you forgive yourself?

Everyone holds on to our past mistakes. Maybe we weren't there for a loved one when they needed us, maybe we blame ourselves for not performing as well as we should in our professional lives. Over time the guilt, and self-blame can become a heavy burden that starts to take a toll on our psychological well being. It is important for us to understand perfection is not possible. We are doing the best we can, to the best of our abilities, and that has to be enough. There is no need for punishing ourselves. Can you imagine how much lighter you would feel If you forgive yourself? How would you go about doing that?

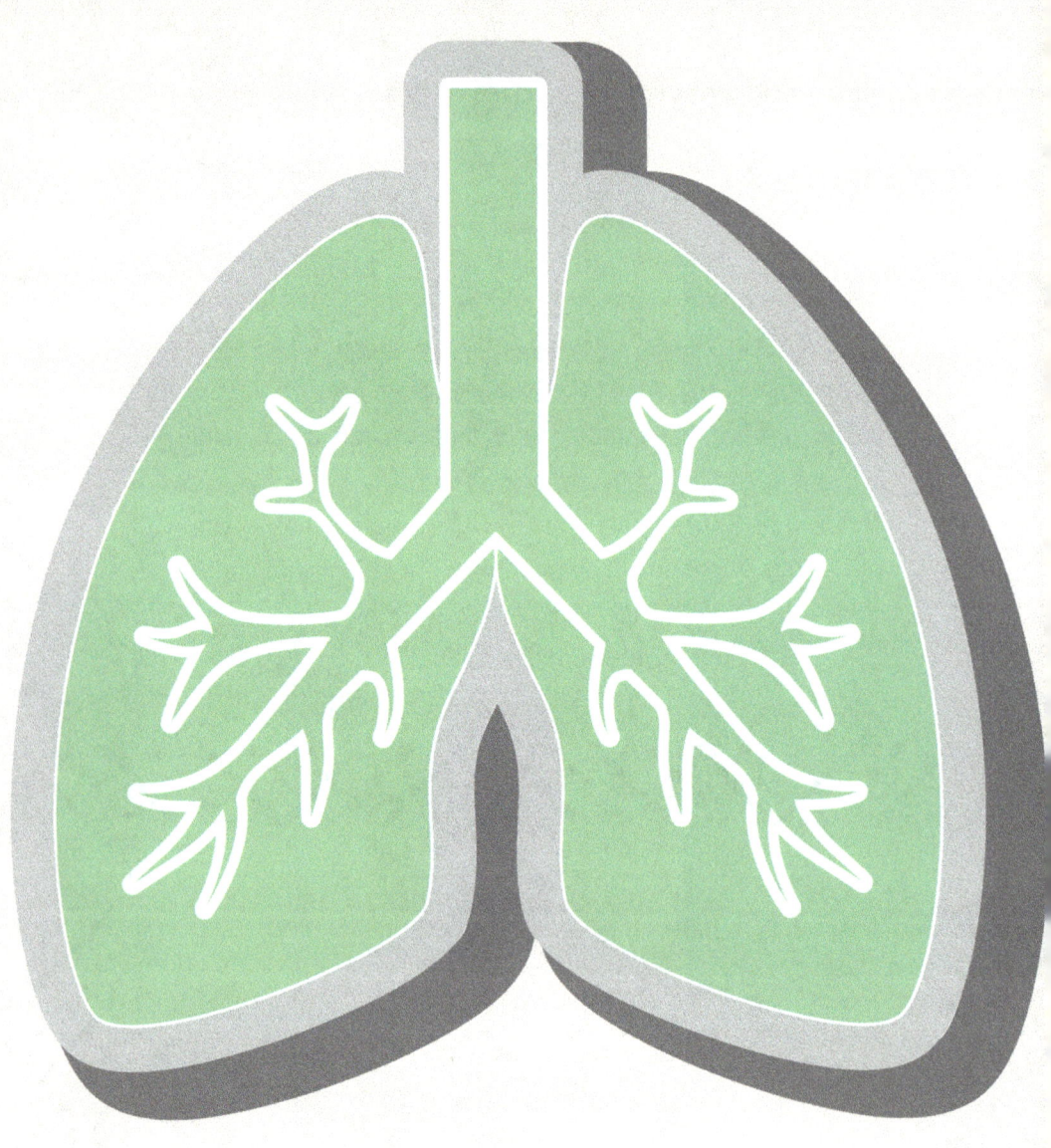

breathe in

DAY 10.

Improve the quality of your life through breathing

The 4-7-8 breathing technique, also known as "relaxing breath," involves breathing in for 4 seconds, holding your breath for 7 seconds, and exhaling for 8 seconds.

Research shows that through breathing techniques your stress levels can drop dramatically, you can also reduce your anxiety level, decrease fatigue, and give your mind and body a sense of wellbeing. No reason not to give it a go!

How do I do it?

Adopt a comfortable seated position before starting and rest the tip of your tongue on the backside of your front teeth.

Breath out until your lungs are empty

Breathe in quietly through the nose for 4 seconds

Hold the breath for 7 seconds

Exhale with force through the mouth, pursing the lips for 8 seconds

Repeat the cycle up to 8-12 times

Start off with doing this exercise 2 times a day. You can do longer rounds the more you do it. If you feel lightheadedness, stop the exercise and rest until you feel better.

IMMUNE BOOSTING TEA

TOTAL TIME: 10 MIN

INGREDIENTS

5 cups of water
Juice of 1 lemon
Peel of 1 lemon
2 inch piece of ginger
cut in smaller pieces
2 inch piece of turmeric
root cut in smaller pieces
Tiny pinch of cayenne
pepper
1 crack of black pepper
1 teaspoon virgin
coconut oil
Honey

DIRECTIONS

Bring the water, lemon peel, ginger, turmeric, cayenne, and black pepper to a bare simmer. Turn the heat down to low and leave for 7 minutes. You don't want the pot to bubble or boil. Take off the heat and squeeze in the lemon juice and stir in the coconut oil. Strain the tea into a cup and add 1 teaspoon of honey. Enjoy hot or cold! Keep in the fridge for up to 3 days.

Daily movement

Movement is great for body and mind. By just adding a few more minutes of movement to your routine every day, your mental health can improve noticeably.

Research shows that exercise stimulates the production of certain chemicals in the brain which energize and elevate your mood. Movement reduces stress, calms your mind, increases energy, and makes it easier for you to relax, sleep, and focus when you need to.

Increase the number of steps you take in a day

Set a goal first! What is the number of steps you want to take in a day? If you feel uncertain in regards to how much this should be, go on your phone and look up how much you are walking today (all smartphones record your daily step count.) Then add 20% and make that your goal. For example, if you are walking 10'000 steps today and your goal is to increase your steps count by 20%, your new goal will then be 12'000 steps daily (10'000 x 1,20 = 12'000).

"You are allowed to be both a masterpiece and a work in progress simultaneously."

-Unknown

Let the creativity flow

Allow yourself to express self-love when it wants to come out (even if you might have to help it to come out sometimes). Do this now by writing a self-love poem or a song about yourself, to yourself.

Share it with someone or keep it to yourself. It might feel a bit unnatural at first, but be open-minded. Creativity and self-love go hand in hand. By opening up to exercises like these you will be far more in tune with yourself, and self-love will start to come naturally!

DAY 13.

this is my jam:

ORGANISE LIKE A

DAY 14.

Having an organized home is rewarding in many ways. You need to clean less, it frees up space and time, that you can use to focus on what you want to.

If you live in clutter and messiness becomes a part of your home, at some point you start looking right past it. Even if you can't see it, however, it does affect your mood, stress levels, tranquility, and focus. By getting rid of the clutter in your home, you are doing yourself a huge favor!

Get a new perspective by imagining that you are a guest in your own home. Imagine you walk in through the door for the first time. What do you see? Take note of what a guest would notice that you simply don't see anymore. If this feels difficult, take photos of your home and look at the photos. Do you now see the paper pile in the kitchen that has been there forever? Do you notice the paintings hanging on the wall creating more of a messy impression, instead of giving the room positivity?

Great!

Now take action and change things up to make things less messy and more harmonious.

YUMMY MUD MASK

**TOTAL TIME:
35 MIN**

INGREDIENTS

2-3 Tablespoons
Greek yogurt
1 tsp. cocoa powder
1 tsp. buttermilk
¼-1/2 of a banana,
mashed
1 tsp. honey
1 tsp. lemon juice

DIRECTIONS

Mix all the ingredients together in a blender. Apply on your face and leave it on for 20-30 minutes. Wash off with cool water to close your pores, leaving your skin feeling super soft. The recipe is enough for 3-4 face masks.
Remember to always do a patch test 24 hours before applying the face mask to your face.

"You were born to be
real, not to be perfect."

- Unknown

Time for questions

What are you holding on to?

What destructive thoughts or beliefs are you carrying around that you know deep down you should let go of?

What would you like to learn?

Learning new things makes us feel good about ourselves. Therefore, learning new things that you enjoy, or think you might enjoy doing, are a brilliant way to increase your sense of well being, and quench the hidden thirst for an adventure deep inside.

Make your life more exciting by coming up with 5 new things you want to try and or learn, write them down, and make time to do them!

Make your home greener

Did you know that plants make us happier? It's true, you feel more relaxed, enhance concentration, and even make your memory better! Buy a plant and take care of it. Soon the plant will take care of you too.

Pro tip - Grow your own plants from seeds

Grow your own plants from seeds. With an egg carton, soil, some light, water, and love your window sill can become an excellent greenhouse for you to enjoy. Some herbs are easy to grow and take care of, and you will see the seeds sprouting fast. Some are good to cook with as well!

I recommend the following if you are a first-time grower:

Parsley	**Chives**
Basil	**Mint**
Lemon grass	**Lemongrass**
Oregano	**Cilantro**

DELICIOUS BANANA CHOCOLATE ICE CREAM

TOTAL TIME: 10 MIN

INGREDIENTS

4 frozen bananas, peeled
1/4 cup cocoa powder
2 tablespoons almond butter (can sub peanut butter)
1/4 cup milk of choice (only use if you are making this in a food processor)

Optional: chocolate chunks or chips, to sprinkle on the top

DIRECTIONS

Use a food processor or a high powered blender, and blend all the ingredients together. Scrape down the ice cream from the edges when needed and process for about 4 minutes or until it turns creamy and ice cream like.

"The real difficulty is to overcome how you think about yourself."

- Maya Angelou

Self esteem

DAY 19.

Not always, but most of the time, practicing self-love can be difficult because of our lack of self-esteem. Being aware of this fact when it hinders our self-love practice, and planning to work through our self-esteem issue is key in our journey towards self-acceptance. The list below consists of a few things that experts think are the most important solutions to our self-esteem issues in life. Think about how you feel towards this list. Are you doing any of them? Could you see yourself incorporating one or more of them in your day to day life?

1. Being mindful, and quieting down the negative thoughts you have about yourself

2. Being open to change and thinking differently, things aren't going to change unless you do or think in new ways

3. Realizing that you are unique and can't be compared to anyone else

4. Taking the time to find out what you are good at and what your strengths are

5. Moving your body to release feel-good chemicals and to stay healthyHelping others

6. Practicing forgiveness

7. Realizing that you are not your circumstances and things will not always stay the same

Enjoy your own company!

DAY 20.

Take yourself out and enjoy being with yourself. Go to a museum, a cinema, a concert, or a play and soak in some culture with the most important person in your life: yourself!

For some people, this feels like an odd thing to do, but a key part of self-love practice is learning to enjoy your own company. In little to no time you will find spending some quality time with yourself to be highly enjoyable and energizing.

Lets get rid of some stuff!

By now you understand that by cleaning out the mess in your home your mood and mind become calmer, more relaxed, and more focused. But even with that knowledge, it can be hard to know exactly where to start and what to clear out. I really don't mean for you to start throwing away items you own and love, I simply want you to start thinking of whether or not you really need ALL of the things you own. With fewer things to move around, clean up, and look at your mind can start focusing on the important stuff instead.

On the next page there is a list of some types of items that can help you think of the unnecessary things in your home, that are only taking up space, and not bringing you any joy whatsoever. Remember to never get rid of things that you love or need, only the things that are not useful for you or giving you any joy. **Good luck!**

DAY 21.

JEWELRY	KITCHEN GLASSWARE
PURSES	COOKBOOKS
PILLOWS	KITCHEN GADGETS
LINEN SETS	KITCHEN APPLIANCES
DUVETS / COMFORTERS	POTS / PANS
BLANKETS	MIXING BOWLS
TOWELS	TUPPERWARE
TELEVISIONS	WATER PITCHERS
ITEMS ON YOUR BULLETIN BOARD	COFFEE MUGS
MAGNETS	GLASS JARS
HOME OFFICE SUPPLIES	MAGAZINES / NEWSPAPERS
COINS	BOOKS
PENS / PENCILS	OVER-THE-COUNTER MEDICINE
RUBBER BANDS / TWIST TIES	MAKE UP
CLEANING SUPPLIES	HAIR ACCESSORIES
OLD BATTERIES	PERSONAL BEAUTY APPLIANCES
TOOLS	TOILETRIES
HARDWARE	PHOTOS
COOLERS	PHOTOGRAPHY SUPPLIES
MANUALS	SEWING SUPPLIES
PHONE BOOKS	SCRAP-BOOKING SUPPLIES
COUPONS	OTHER CRAFT SUPPLIES
BOARD GAMES	CDS
PUZZLES	DVDS / VHS TAPES
DECKS OF CARDS	WALL DECORATIONS
UNUSED GIFTS	CANDLES
BABY CLOTHES	CANDLE HOLDERS
BABY SUPPLIES	FIGURINES
OLD SCHOOLBOOKS/PAPERS	CRYSTAL / CHINA
TOYS	VASES
STUFFED ANIMALS	AUDIO/VISUAL COMPONENTS
KID'S ARTWORK	AUDIO/VISUAL CABLES
SUITCASES	COMPUTERS EQUIPMENT
PANTRY FOOD	COMPUTER PERIPHERALS
PAPER GOODS	OLD CELLPHONES
WRAPPING SUPPLIES	FURNITURE
PET SUPPLIES	VIDEO GAME SYSTEMS
PLASTIC BAGS	VIDEO GAME ACCESSORIES
PARTY SUPPLIES	VIDEO GAMES
SEASONAL DECORATIONS	SHIRTS
SPORTING GOODS	PANTS / SHORTS
SPORTS MEMORABILIA	DRESSES / SKIRTS
AUTOMOBILES	HATS
AUTOMOTIVE SUPPLIES	CLOTHES HANGERS
SCRAP PIECES OF LUMBER	SHOES
BROOMS	TIES / BELTS / ACCESSORIES
RAKES	COATS
SHOVELS	WINTER GEAR
GARDEN TOOLS	SOCKS / UNDERWEAR
PLANT CONTAINERS / POTS	SLEEPWEAR

HEALING AND FIZZY FOOTBATH

**TOTAL TIME:
25 MIN**

INGREDIENTS

3tbs of baking soda
3 cups of warm water,
as hot as you like
without burning yourself
The juice of half a
lemon
½ cup of Epsom salt

DIRECTIONS

Combine all the ingredients and let your feet soak in the footbath for 15-20 minutes. Epsom salt is loaded with magnesium which is easily absorbed through your skin and leaves your feet feeling smooth and your body relaxed. You can not believe how relaxing and awesome a nice footbath is! I dare you to not fall in love with doing it.

"No one can make you feel

inferior without your consent."

- Eleanor Roosevelt

Time for some thinking

How can you spice up your life?

Sometimes we get stuck in a rut, in old habits and routines so it can be quite beneficial to change things up from time to time. How can you do that now? Would you like to cook more? Get a new friend? Go on a date? Spend more time with yourself? Write down all the things that come to mind, and execute!

_____

_____

_____

_____

_____

_____

DAY 23.

How can you pamper yourself today?

It is important to take care of yourself and listen to what you want. Having some time for yourself once a day or once a week can improve your quality of life in surprising ways. You just might learn new things about yourself too. Think of what you enjoy doing, pick a way to pamper yourself, and set aside a time and a day to regularly do exactly that! You deserve it.

EXPLORE MEDITATION

The benefits of meditation are endless. It is not a coincidence that more and more people are learning and practicing meditation. From singer, songwriters, to silicon valley execs, and Elon Musk meditation is all the rage now! A common obstacle for people trying to pick up meditation is often the overcomplicated way that it is taught. At first glance, most people think you will need years of practice before you can meditate. We are here to tell you that, that perception is false. Everyone can do it, and it is not even that difficult.

Meditation can reduce stress, anxiety, generate kindness, enhance self-awareness, may help to fight off addictions, boosts your immune system, and can reduce pain. Well, the list goes on. So in my opinion, it seems silly to not even give it a try at least.

How to meditate

- Sit down in a comfortable position

- Wear comfortable clothes

- Eyes closed

- Relax your body

- Let your thought drift away as they come up

- Focus on your breathing

Keep it short if you are a beginner and focus on getting some consistency instead. If you are struggling with letting your thoughts drift away, put on a free guided meditation that you can find on youtube to make the process easier. Guided meditations are awesome and super easy to do! **Namaste.**

"In order to love who you are,
you cannot hate the experiences
that shaped you."

- Andréa Dykstra

DELICIOUS AND QUICK ENERGY BALLS

**TOTAL TIME:
1 HOUR 30 MIN**

INGREDIENTS

1 cup old-fashioned oats
2/3 cup toasted shredded coconut (sweetened or unsweetened)
1/2 cup creamy peanut butter
1/2 cup ground flaxseed
1/2 cup semisweet chocolate chips (or vegan chocolate chips)
1/3 cup honey
1 tablespoon chia seeds (optional)
1 teaspoon vanilla extract

DIRECTIONS

Mix all the ingredients together in a large bowl. Let the mix chill in the fridge for about an hour or until the mixture is properly chilled. Roll the mix into 1 inch balls. Enjoy immediately or keep in the fridge for up to 1 week to enjoy later.

Pro tips: you can also make a big batch of energy balls and freeze them for up to 3 months. Take them out 1 hour before eating to let them thaw. When you are having a healthy good alternative to other snacks it is much more likely you will choose the more healthy one. Especially when they are incredibly delicious.

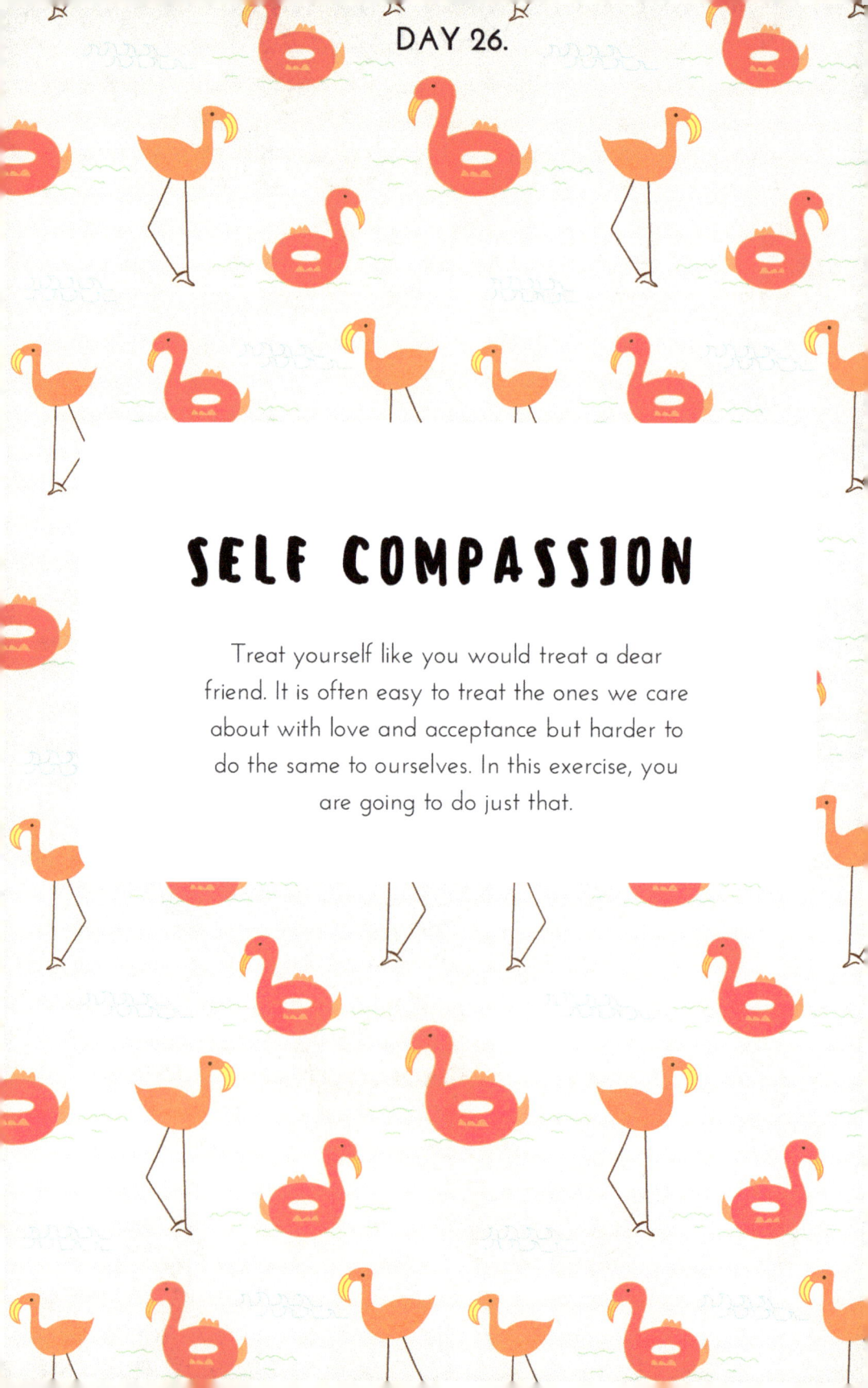

SELF COMPASSION

Treat yourself like you would treat a dear friend. It is often easy to treat the ones we care about with love and acceptance but harder to do the same to ourselves. In this exercise, you are going to do just that.

DAY 26.

Imagine a specific friend that you hold dear. He or she is feeling bad and struggling in some way. Try and think of a specific problem that might have happened or could happen to your friend. Write down how you would act and respond to your friend in this situation.

Now imagine yourself in a similar situation, when you feel bad and are struggling. Write down how you respond to yourself, what do you think to yourself, and how do you act?

Compare the two notes you just made. What are the differences? Now ask yourself why there is a difference.

Imagine how much better life would be if you would treat yourself with the same respect you had towards your friend. What implications do you think that would have? How would things be different?

Keep a happy journal

DAY 27.

Having a creative outlet can be helpful in many ways, some research even shows that its effects can be as amazing as meditation! Being creative calms your mind, can reduce stress, and can even work as a natural antidepressant. Also, it is a lot of fun!

Instead of keeping a journal, keep a happy creative journal that you fill with drawings, happy memories, beautiful and inspiring quotes, whatever you want, that are fun and help you get in a good mood. A great way to start can be searching online for inspiration.

You don't have to write or draw something every day in your journal, just when you feel like it. Think of it as a quick pick me up.

Declutter your phone

If you live in the modern world, your phone is probably a big part of your life. It's your way to stay connected to your friends and family, to find out what is going on in the world, your phone is basically an extension of you.

For the amount of time we are spending on our phones, it is strange that the idea of decluttering your phone is not more common. Is it always easy to find what you are looking for? Are you subscribed to email lists that you don't really care about? It is time to do something about that now. Here are 6 easy things for you to do right now to have a more decluttered phone.

1. Update your contact list, and delete old ones
2. Delete apps you are not using
3. Create folders based on color or function
4. Backup your photos and content on the cloud and delete on your phone
5. Unsubscribe from email lists
6. Delete old emails

Resources

BijanBijan Kholghi is a life coach with special psychological education in hypno-systemic coaching. His teacher Dr. Gunther Schmidt is the founder of Milton Erickson Institute in Heidelberg (Germany). (2020, May 20). 25 Boosting Self Esteem Questions. Retrieved August 19, 2020, from https://www.coaching-online.org/self-esteem-questions/

Resnick, N. (2018, July 19). 5 Scientific Reasons Decluttering Your Home Will Make You Happier. Retrieved August 19, 2020, from https://thriveglobal.com/stories/5-scientific-reasons-decluttering-your-home-will-make-you-happier/

4-7-8 breathing: How it works, benefits, and uses. (n.d.). Retrieved August 19, 2020, from https://www.medicalnewstoday.com/articles/324417

5 Health Benefits of Daily Meditation According to Science. (2020, May 18). Retrieved August 19, 2020, from https://positivepsychology.com/benefits-of-meditation/

7 Most Effective Self-Esteem Tools and Activities. (2020, March 12). Retrieved August 19, 2020, from https://positivepsychology.com/self-esteem-tools-activities/

What Do We Mean By Self-Love - Dr. Andrea Brandt. (2018, March 29). Retrieved August 19, 2020, from https://abrandtherapy.com/what-do-we-mean-when-we-say-self-love/

Thank you